THE DRAGONFLY WORKSHEETS

Supporting Key Stage 2 and 3 Dyslexic Pupils, their Teachers and Support Staff

'I have found Sally Raymond's worksheets ideally suited for use with pupils in need of focused literacy development materials. They find them varied and accessible with opportunities to include personal interests and topics. I use them to match specific learning needs to activities which introduce, explain, engage and assess individual targets and skills.' – *Julia Smith BEd, SpLD, APC (Patoss) dyslexia assessor and tutor*

Dragonfly Worksheets resource book provides all the materials required to follow structured programmes of learning support for dyslexic pupils. Created by Sally Raymond, an experienced teacher of dyslexic pupils, this resource provides a wide variety of adaptable worksheets with lots of teaching advice and supportive guidance.

The worksheets:

- fully adapted to meet the needs of different pupils
- support Department for Education recommendations and Ofsted advice and guidance
- encourage cross-curricula support and interventions to promote maximum access to a wide range of topics
- use varied, enjoyable applications including games, quizzes and novel challenges designed to engage and stimulate thinking and learning
- develop the knowledge and skills of practitioners helping them identify and monitor progress and needs.

Also available by Sally Raymond:

Extending Support for Key Stage 2 and 3 Dyslexic Pupils, their Teachers and Support Staff: The Dragonfly Games (Routledge, 2015), and *Spelling Rules, Riddles and Remedies* (Routledge, 2014).

Sally Raymond DipSpLD(Hornsby), PGDip(SEN) is an experienced dyslexia tutor and trainer living in Cornwall.

Second edition published 2015
by Routledge
2 Park Square, Milton Park, Abingdon, Oxon OX14 4RN

and by Routledge
711 Third Avenue, New York, NY 10017

Routledge is an imprint of the Taylor & Francis Group, an informa business

© 2015 Sally Raymond

First edition published 2001 by Routledge

Trademark notice: Product or corporate names may be trademarks or registered trademarks, and are used only for identification and explanation without intent to infringe.

British Library Cataloguing in Publication Data
A catalogue record for this book is available from the British Library

Library of Congress Cataloging in Publication Data
A catalog record for this title has been requested

ISBN: 978-1-138-77461-2 (hbk)
ISBN: 978-1-138-77462-9 (pbk)
ISBN: 978-1-315-75226-6 (ebk)

Typeset in Bembo
by Book Now Ltd, London

Contents

Summary of Application

- Read through the 'Teaching advice' section.

- Introduce the Dragonfly Worksheet alongside the pupil(s).

- Enhance the lesson inputs by using additional resources (e.g. wooden letters) and practise answers in a 'jottings' notebook (supplied to each pupil for use in class).

- Ask the pupil to complete the worksheet for homework.

- Review the material in the following lesson.

- Create new worksheets.

- Monitor progress and collate record sheets.

Introduction

Dragonfly Worksheets presents a variety of engaging topics and activities for use with learners to develop their reading, spelling and writing abilities. They provide engaging, flexible, focused, structured and memory-friendly teaching and learning resources.

Each sample worksheet is accompanied by 'teaching advice' which describes their design and delivery. This promotes an understanding of the style and purpose of specialised teaching techniques to enable both experienced and inexperienced teachers to deliver Dragonfly Worksheets. 'Adaptive possibilities' further extend the scope of the worksheets by encouraging the use of personalisation and variety to match individual learning needs. By using cross-curricula and extension materials, learners develop confidence, knowledge and skills as they follow a structured progression through topics selected by their teachers.

The following are just some of the influential guidelines in place as this book is prepared for its latest reprint:

- Sir Jim Rose's report *Identifying and Teaching Children and Young People with Dyslexia and Literacy Difficulties* (June 2009) demonstrates the need for all practitioners to have access to specialist teaching materials.
- MPs informing government policy through an All-Party Parliamentary Group's *Inquiry into Overcoming the Barriers to Literacy* (July 2011) highlights the necessity for teachers to select resources for literacy to suit individual needs.
- *Support and Aspiration: A New Approach to Special Educational Needs and Disability* (DfE 2012) champions the development of the knowledge and skills of teachers and other learning-support staff.
- The Ofsted Framework (2012) calls for evidence of well-targeted and effective interventions which also inform assessment and progress.
- In April 2013, Ofsted published a report entitled *Improving Literacy in Secondary Schools: A Shared Responsibility* which recommends an emphasis on practical ideas that teachers can use in longer term plans and schemes of work. It also emphasises the need for literacy development to occur across all subjects within the curriculum to improve pupils' self-esteem, motivation, behaviour, independence and attainment.
- In 2014, the new National Curriculum English programme of study promotes ambitious goals for as many children as possible to achieve. Alongside a stimulating curriculum which aspires to foster a love of education for its own sake, the focus on school accountability will require evidence-based examples of delivery methods and outcomes.

Application

Having selected an appropriate worksheet (along with vocabulary to suit the learner's requirements), a focused and shared exploration of the worksheet is undertaken, led by the teacher, utilising any additional learning aids (such as wooden letters, coloured pens and links to a previous topic). Discussion and investigation should be encouraged as the learner practises the application of different skills within a supportive environment. This helps to remove anxiety and stress, stimulates the priming of key topics, and ensures a clarity of purpose and expectations.

The learner is then given a new copy of the worksheet which they complete (with or without support, according to need), as a follow-on activity.

This pattern of application (prepare, practise and then repeat) suits the needs of the dyslexic learner, who often finds that the handling of literacy-based material triggers working-memory overload, leading to a failure to assimilate lesson objectives and outcomes. By pacing inputs and by priming the key ingredients of an activity, access to the rewards of success is increased. Repetition also promotes the development of stronger memory traces. The continuation of a worksheet's theme by revisiting its design at a future date with new terminology and/or topic further builds on the foundations of skills and knowledge to stimulate a progression of ability and achievement of targets.

Planning and monitoring

A comprehensive index is provided (page 119) which details specific aspects contained in Worksheets A–Z (and subsequent extensions). Teachers can use this index to plan individualised teaching programmes of support.

Once worksheets have been selected, differentiated and reproduced, they await introduction in files allocated to individual pupils.

Pupil record sheets (see pages 8–11) allow teachers to record pupil application and provides information for the production of further worksheets. This helps to evidence interventions and achievement as well as identifying areas in need of future targeted attention.

Filing further worksheets

As new worksheets are created from the templates provided in this book to produce individualised programmes of support, it is suggested they are labelled according to their original source (e.g. worksheet P2, P3, etc.). This allows extension worksheets to be collated alongside the Contents list at the front of Dragonfly Worksheets, as well as relating to the key topic index on page 119.

This method of collating worksheets makes it easier for practitioners and assessors to identify and track areas of study completed by individual pupils.

Meeting the Needs of Dyslexic Pupils

Dyslexia affects the acquisition of language, mostly in its written form, although spoken expression can be affected too.

Reading, written composition, spelling and numeracy are commonly found to contain errors despite adequate access to learning. Sequences such as multiplication tables, the calendar months and instructions are frequently forgotten or disordered, with the effect of these early difficulties further influencing the developmental progress of the dyslexic child.

Dyslexic pupils vary enormously. Neurological processes (based primarily in the visual, audio, semantic and kinesthetic centres of the brain) harbour different levels of weakness or strength, which affect the individual's capacity and style of learning approach. This accounts for one dyslexic pupil achieving reading skills through visual-processing strengths, and then being unable to recount the meaning of words through weaknesses in the semantic (word meanings) centres of their brain. Another pupil may lack visual-processing skills. This leads to an over-reliance on audio factors and a reading style where even familiar words are broken down into individual letters or letter clusters rather than visually recognised as a whole.

Underlying the learning, retention and recall of language is the memory. Not only are individual memory centres (visual, audio, etc.) and the processes involved with short-term to long-term memory transference required to be effective, but the capacity of the working memory to cope with the merger of inputs and outputs needs to be able to meet the demands of the task in hand. Reading involves a variety of memory skills (visual and audio along with ocular scanning); to read aloud adds vocal skills to the processing challenge; to comprehend the text requires access to semantic memory traces; and then prediction, reiteration and retention of information involve further processing challenges. Successful reading is by no means a simple achievement!

Along with individual memory-processing weaknesses, the overloading of working memory frequently causes a reduction in the learning and performance ability of dyslexic pupils. Dragonfly Worksheets are specifically designed to present information in manageable chunks with numerous opportunities for revision and experience that improves both the quality and security of long-term memory traces. Rather than expecting reading, writing or memory skills, etc. to be achieved through one lesson, the programme of worksheets contains varied examples of spelling, reading and applicational experience. Through the delivery style (worksheets introduced alongside a teacher) and their delayed application (worksheets completed for homework), along with reviews the following lesson and further delivery of worksheet variations, dyslexic pupils receive little, often, repetitive and varied inputs that suit their learning style and address the specific areas of weakness found within the dyslexic profile(s).

Support Throughout the Curriculum

Support for dyslexic pupils traditionally occurs during English lessons through individual or small group withdrawal sessions. However, dyslexic pupils also require support throughout the school day when handling topics such as French, history, science and mathematics. They need help identifying novel terminology, understanding diagrammatic displays and achieving reading and writing success. They need teachers who understand their specific weaknesses and strengths, who tailor inputs to avoid working memory overload, provide interesting and varied repetition, and deliver encouraging praise and reasonable expectations. The dyslexic pupil can neither understand the details of dyslexia nor express their needs in the way we would expect from a child with a broken leg, so adults concerned with their academic and pastoral care need information and guidelines to support discovery.

Each Dragonfly Worksheet is accompanied by 'Teaching advice' that enables inexperienced teachers of dyslexic pupils to understand the method of delivery and nature of input covered. 'Adaptive possibilities' highlight ways that worksheet templates can be used to support specific subjects: history quizzes, French vocabulary, geographic terminology, memory games and written tasks all enhance the skills dyslexic pupils need to achieve to succeed. The creation, delivery and appraisal of worksheets develop teachers' understanding of their pupils' needs, enhancing their teaching ability, assessment of progress and target setting.

As further worksheets extend the Dragonfly Worksheets in this book into a library of applications, the potential for support throughout the school day becomes an achievable goal.

Processing Weaknesses Found Within the Dyslexic Profile

All dyslexic pupils have different weaknesses and strengths.

	Examples of processing skills reduced by these weaknesses	Nature of specific inputs
Weaknesses within the **audio** modality	Audio memory Phonic reading decoding skills Spelling Tables	Audio memory exercises Focus on phonetics Single-word decoding Spelling families
Weaknesses within the **visual** modality	Visual memory Decoding of visual displays Spelling	Visual memory exercises Focus on visual displays Whole-word reading Spelling oddities
Semantic weaknesses	Word-finding difficulties Word meaning weaknesses Associated word prompting low	Reading comprehension Written compositions Thesaurus and root words Word association tasks Processing speed
Kinesthetic weaknesses	Penmanship Copying Left-to-right visual scanning	Hand-to-eye control Differentiation needs Copying skills
Additional weaknesses	Organisation Self-esteem Memory loss	Work filing system Achievable tasks Understanding and revision

Organisation of Delivery

In order for material to be delivered and monitored effectively, a number of additional resources are required (denoted by ★ below).

Dragonfly Worksheets are intended for delivery in class alongside a teacher, followed by their completion for homework. This approach encourages the transfer of material from short-term memory into long-term memory, as pupils are required, in effect, to do the work twice.

If worksheets are completed in class, pupils need only utilise short-term memory and can then readily forget the details of the work that was covered. Requiring the completion of the worksheets for homework develops stronger long-term memory traces through the process of memory recall.

- Photocopy selected Dragonfly Worksheets in advance and store them in a storage folder★ (kept within the school) assigned to the pupil. List the enclosed worksheets on the folder's cover, applying a tick when worksheets have been presented. This allows for advanced planning.
- Introduce worksheets alongside the pupil, practising application in a jottings notebook★. Spellings can be practised in this notebook using colour to highlight patterns and oddities. Pictures can be added to reinforce inputs (such as drawing a world in place of the 'o' in 'world' to highlight the oddity of its spelling). Spelling analogies can be collected (e.g. 'honey' and 'money'), and sentences/ answers can be practised during lesson time. This notebook is retained by the teacher, requiring pupils to recall lesson inputs rather than copy them. Additional resources★ (wooden letters, coloured pens, etc.) should also be used to support learning.
- Pupil record sheets★ (see pages 8–11) enable teachers to record and monitor worksheet delivery and comment on individual progress. The spellings checklist (pages 12–13) provides information for further worksheets and records the coverage of spelling needs.
- Place current worksheet(s) in the pupil's homework folder★ for transportation, including any reading book and diary★ for home/school communication, etc. if required.
- Store completed worksheets in a performance folder★, enabling teachers to measure application over time.
- As further worksheets are created they can be stored in a file of plastic wallets★, displayed alphabetically in order to match the master index of Dragonfly Worksheets (p. 119).

Pupil Record Sheet

Name: _____ **Date of birth:** _____ **Class:** _____ **Term:** _____

Reading needs	Spelling needs	Writing composition	Penmanship	Numeracy	Memory	Other
Worksheets:	*Worksheets:*	*Worksheets:*	*Worksheets:*	*Worksheets:*	*Worksheets:*	*Worksheets:*

Spelling errors: _____

Reading errors: _____

Pupil Record Sheet (page 2)

Date of lesson	Worksheet(s)	Application of worksheet	Further needs

Pupil Record Sheet Example

Name: Mark Collard   **Date of birth:** 8/8/2004   **Class:** 5DS   **Term:** Summer 2013

Reading needs	Spelling needs	Writing composition	Penmanship	Numeracy	Memory	Other
Decoding errors: poor chunking skills. Comprehension weak.	Spells using sounds (kat). Long-term memory poor.	Lack of punctuation. Expression poor. Length short.	b/d confusion. Oversized, irregular letters.	Symbolic confusion (×/+). Language confusion (times/multiply).	Audio memory weaknesses. Visual memory weaknesses.	Good verbal expression. Youngest of three siblings.
Worksheets: A, G, H, I, J, N, Q, T, W, Y,	Worksheets: B, C, F, M, S, Z,	Worksheets: G, L, O, T, U,	Worksheets: G, M, U, S, O, L,	Worksheets: P, Q, V,	Worksheets: D, E, H, K, P, X,	Worksheets:

Spelling errors: house/hows, will/wil, does/dose, hopping/hoping,

smile/smil, they're/there, their/there, rabbit/rabet, time/tim,

poor/por, teacher/ticher, nice/nic, discovery/discuvry, jumped/jumpt,

hair/har

Reading errors: when/then, was/saw, church/chick, lady/lad,

contain/continue, sleeps/sleep, weave/wave, draw/born.

Guesses words by appearance: not using context or phonic decoding.

Interest level above reading achievement Level. Minimal use of

pictorial prompts. Use finger to help tracking.

© 2015, Supporting Key Stage 2 and 3 Dyslexic Pupils, their Teachers and Support Staff: The Dragonfly Worksheets, 2nd edition, Sally Raymond, Routledge.

Pupil Record Sheet Example (page 2)

If you number the pages in the pupil's file, the cross-referencing of comments, activities and recommendations are easier to follow. This aids planning, assessment and report-writing.

Date of lesson	Worksheet(s)	Application of worksheet	Further needs
Wednesday 24th April 2013 1.30–1.45pm	E: homophones. Read through words (with support) and discuss meaning. Create a storyline for each block of words and link to a picture. Complete page 2 in class and again for homework. Resources: E1 worksheet side 1 (2 copies); individual word-cards sorted into groups; Bingo cards; 4 pictures (A to D); pens, notebook; spelling booklet; E1 worksheet side 2 (2 copies)	Reason for worksheet: Memory of homophones weak; spelling errors and poor reading comprehension. Use pictures A to D to link to different story-lines: A: road; B: horse (rode); C: witch; D: twins (which one?) _Single-word reading and comprehension (with support): useful activity._ _Highlights weak whole-word recognition / reliance on phonic decoding._ _Struggled on spelling patterns such as 'pour' 'guest' 'sew'._ _Creative ideas – excellent verbal contributions (exceeds creative writing performance); opportunity to over-learn the different spelling to meaning links (very useful). Moved individual word-cards about as invented story-line (encouraged M. to use whole-word recognition if possible – M. pleased when recognised words correctly)._ _The verbalising words in context allowed assessment of comprehension – good understanding of word-meaning within this context._ _M. given time to sketch own pictures in his notebook to match the 'road' and 'rode' story-lines to each block of words. Verbalising and then labelled the use of different words._ _Completed page 2 in class – used coloured pens to highlight spelling patterns and, for those he struggled with, added a further link e.g. toad in the road and the best guest wore a vest. Enjoyed making these extra links even though they were not always needed._ _Played two games of Bingo (setting out game provided good opportunity for a change of activity). Added 'pour' to spelling booklet (pour out Uncle's rum)._ _Homework appraisal: Completed worksheet accurately. Reported the use of 'through / threw' needed help. Pleased to have completed challenge successfully._	Next session: read Bingo cards. Revisit the verbalisation of story-lines using each block of words. At future session: Repeat activity using a selection of these words along with new ones to revise, reinforce and extend. (Create Worksheets E2 and E3 using extension vocabulary.) Prepare a copy of Worksheet A to include homophones covered in Worksheet E to revise the topic (alongside other material which is covered this half term). Assess memory and application. Encourage and discuss the use of homophones in mainstream reading and writing activities. Evaluate reading, comprehension and spelling skills through use of Worksheet F: 'Quiz time', e.g. What is the opposite of 'right'? What is the hair on a horse's neck called?; 'A welcomed sight is often called a sight for ……… eyes.'

Spellings Checklist

Enter details of spelling inputs delivered (e.g. -dg-: bridge, fridge (18/09/01), edge, hedge (25/09/01); B3 -dg- words (25/01/01). Cross off those that become fully internalised.

Name: _____ **Date:** _____

sh/th/ch: _____

_____

Short vowels: _____

_____

Long vowels: _____

_____

Alphabet: letter sounds: _____ sequence: _____

Consonant blends

ar: _____   -ck: _____

_____   _____

-ly: _____   kn-: _____

_____   _____

er: ir: ur: _____   wr-: _____

_____   _____

all: _____   gn-: _____

_____   _____

or: _____   -ed: _____

_____   _____

-ll: _____   o = u: _____
_____   (e.g. 'monkey') _____

-ss: _____   or = er: _____
_____   (e.g. 'work') _____

-zz: _____   soft c: _____

_____   _____

-ff: _____   soft g: _____

_____   _____

a: _____   k-: _____
(e.g. 'grass') _____   _____

j-: _____

_____

-dg-: _____

_____

-tch: _____

_____

ai/ay: _____

_____

ao: _____

_____

ow: _____

_____

oo: _____
(e.g. 'book') _____

oo: _____
(e.g. 'moon') _____

-igh-: _____

_____

ee: _____

_____

ea: _____

_____

oi/oy: _____

_____

ou: _____

_____

au: _____
(e.g. 'author') _____

y>i: _____

_____

-le: _____

_____

-our: _____
(e.g. 'colour') _____

ch: _____
(e.g. 'choir') _____

-que: _____
(e.g. 'unique') _____

ph: _____

_____

Suffixes: _____

_____

_____

Double consonants: _____

_____

_____

Homophones: _____

_____

_____

Prefixes: _____

_____

_____

Plurals: _____

_____

_____

Oddities (e.g. 'said'): _____

_____

_____

Penmanship: _____

Personal spellings (e.g. names of pets, etc.): _____

_____

_____

Address, telephone number, date of birth: _____

_____

_____

The Dragonfly Worksheets

Worksheet A
Single-word Reading and Comprehension

Teaching advice

Single-word reading exercises employ and develop word decoding skills. The element of contextual guesswork is removed, but by categorising words comprehension is encouraged.

Dyslexic children have weak word-decoding skills. They often exhibit weaknesses associating words through meaning, reducing their reading, compositional skills, word-finding abilities and expression. Variations of Worksheet A extend proficiency.

Worksheet A also practises kinesthetic application (drawing lines), along with short-term visual and semantic memory skills.

In class

Read through batches of words. Support decoding skills by encouraging segmentation of words such as 'policeman'. Note the spelling patterns of words such as 'ice' (soft c), double consonants in 'kitten', 'curry' and 'swimming' but not 'paper', and highlight the spelling of 'piece' (if 'ie/ei' rule has been covered). 'Pleasant' is a sight word as its pronunciation does not match letter-to-sound rules, 'unpleasant' makes use of the prefix 'un-' in order to denote inverted meaning. Identify areas of difficulty.

Note that 'swimming pool' can be assigned to both 'child' and 'adult'.

Encourage pupil(s) to put words into meaningful sentences to ensure comprehension. Ensure that the applicational instructions are understood. Review the completed exercise in the following lesson.

Worksheet A
Single-word Reading and Comprehension

Adaptive possibilities

- **Opposites:** young old   angry happy   big small   black white

- **Spelling patterns:** clothing   pocket
  (e.g. -ck rule)   jacket
                          noise   racket
                                     cluck

- **Historical knowledge:** nineteenth century   Napoleon Bonaparte
                            eighteenth century   The Cold War
                                                 Tolpuddle Martyrs
                                                 Suffragettes

- **Invented words:** water   splashy
  (phonic decoding)   plip plip plip
                       glue   gloopy
                               yicky

- **Decision-making:** like   school
  (choice of association)   football
                        dislike cabbage
                                 Fridays

- **Pupil application:** yellow   ....
  (pupil creates worksheet)   ....
                          blue   ....

Worksheet A1
Single-word Reading and Comprehension

Name:...

Date:... Form:.........................

Draw lines to match words on the right with those on the left.

hot	Africa
	ice-cream
	iced tea
	curry
cold	Arctic
	freezer

man-made	coffee bean
	coffee cup
	shoes
	Africa
	ice
natural	ice-cream
	paper

boy's name	Jonathon
	Jennifer
	James
	Christopher
girl's name	Christine
	Charles

child	grandma
	policeman
	rattle
	playground
adult	swimming pool
	kitten

singular	policemen
	coffee beans
	pair of glasses
	pair of candlesticks
plural	babies
	piece of paper

living	earwig
	policeman
	coffee cup
	kitten
non-living	rock
	piece of paper

kind	pleasant
	unpleasant
	thoughtful
	thoughtless
unkind	policeman
	burglar

Worksheet B
Matching Spellings

Teaching advice

Spelling by analogy helps to develop letter-to-sound patterns. This worksheet helps the pupil to focus on the groups of letters responsible for making up different sounds. It also provides reading experience, exercising reading comprehension skills.

By analysing letter-to-sound relationships, pupils are encouraged to use this approach when faced with an unknown spelling rather than attempting a visual recreation, which is much harder for the reader to decode; for example, 'weard' is easier to decode than 'wird'. Almost all dyslexics face difficulties with spelling so it is necessary to equip them with useful tactics to fall back on.

Letter-to-sound patterns also support reading decoding skills.

In class

Read the instructions together (reading instructions is an important exercise that many dyslexic pupils miss out in favour of guesswork). Read through the key sentence. Analyse words such as 'cried', discussing the interaction of different letters. Then read the following sentences, ensuring that the meaning is understood, and allow the pupil to speak a word to fill each space that shares a letter-to-sound pattern found within the key sentence. Remind the pupil of their need to draw a line (freehand) between words as they complete the worksheet unaided at home. When the sheet is reviewed at the next lesson, a failure to draw lines illustrates their failure to read/remember instructions.

Worksheet B
Matching Spellings

Adaptive possibilities

By analysing pupils' spelling errors, weaknesses in their spelling vocabulary can be strengthened through application.

Familiarise pupils with novel terminology by using material from mainstream curriculum topics that are being covered.

Fields are found in rural areas.

(a) 'Babies' is the..of 'baby'.

Here the meaning of 'rural' and 'plural' is reinforced.

(b) What is the opposite of 'silence'?..

Here a choice of 'noise' is often made, but there is no matching pattern in the key sentence. Pupils need to apply thesaurus skills to come up with 'sound', and then remember this option.

Use words that share a sound, but use a choice of spelling patterns, so that pupils must determine between the two:

The white donkey walks with a slight limp.

(a) Nocturnal animals are awake at..

(b) The cutting action of teeth is called a..

Uncover the letter-to-sound patterns of foreign languages by presenting simple exercises that support mainstream learning.

Worksheet B1
Matching Spellings

Name:..

Date:.. Form:..........................

Fill in the spaces and draw a line to connect that word with the spelling pattern in the *key sentence*.

The little boy sat down on a chair and cried.

1. Something that grows out of your head: ....

2. Something you boil water in: ....

3. Eggs can be boiled, poached, scrambled or...............

4. A baby's toy that makes a noise when it is shaken is called a ....

5. He did not tell the truth, he ....

6. 'It isn't ...., my brother always gets to stay up later than me.'

7. The colour of bark: ....

He threw the spear with all his might.

1. People who work on a ship are called the ....

2. The opposite of 'day' is ....

3. The party was held in the village ....

4. The number that follows two is ....

5. The opposite of 'dark' is ....

6. The opposite of 'old' is ....

7. The past tense of 'know' is ....

8. The part of your body that listens: ....

9. A drop of water that falls from your eye: ....

10. The opposite of 'short' is ....

11. Tim .... away the dirty plates off the table.

Worksheet C
SPATS – A Game Using Short Vowel Sounds

Teaching advice

The term 'short' vowel sound refers to the sound made by a vowel in words such as 'ran' and 'hop'. A second vowel, either directly following the first (e.g. 'rain') or separated from it by one letter (e.g. 'hope') creates a 'long' vowel sound. Therefore, an ability to hear and identify vowel sounds supports spelling ability, explaining and prompting the use of: double consonants (e.g. 'hopping' rather than 'hoping'), which are needed to retain a short vowel sound; the presence of secondary vowels (e.g. 'toad' rather than 'tod'); and the presence of 'ck' following a short vowel sound (e.g. 'pack'). The words 'park' and 'take' do not use 'c', whereas 'speckle' and 'locked' do, due to the presence of a preceding short vowel sound.

Dyslexic pupils often find the identification of vowel sounds difficult. SPATS provides an enjoyable and repetitive game that develops short vowel sound recognition and usage. A prompt card should be used until proficiency is reached, providing pictorial images that reinforce learning.

a: cat	e: egg	i: pin	o: cot	u: mug

Prompt card

In class

Prepare for the game. Play it once in class then provide further copies of page 1 of the worksheet for the game to be repeated at home. Make further worksheets for holiday fun and future revision of short vowel sounds.

Worksheet C
SPATS – A Game Using Short Vowel Sounds

Adaptive possibilities

Whole-class play

Duplicate and distribute a variety of game cards using the examples given and/or creating additional ones. Players take turns to throw the vowel dice (but make a new one repeating 'u' instead of having SPATS on the sixth face). All players then attempt to use this vowel to create a word. Continue until someone has correctly transformed all of their game cards into words.

The second part of the game reinforces the hearing and reading of short vowel sounds. One player reads out one of their words (e.g. 'chip'). If any of the other players has created the same word, all players with that word turn that game card face down. If no other player has the same word the game card is put to one side, face up, and the player who created this word is awarded one point. For a large number of players, adapt this rule to say that a point is awarded for words that only two (three, four) other players have created.

Comment on the correct spellings of errors such as 'sund' ('he sunned himself on the beach') if they arise, and the pronunciation of words such as 'put'.

When all words have been considered, the player(s) with the most points wins.

Worksheet C1
SPATS – A Game Using Short Vowel Sounds

Name:..

Date:.. Form:..........................

Game cards

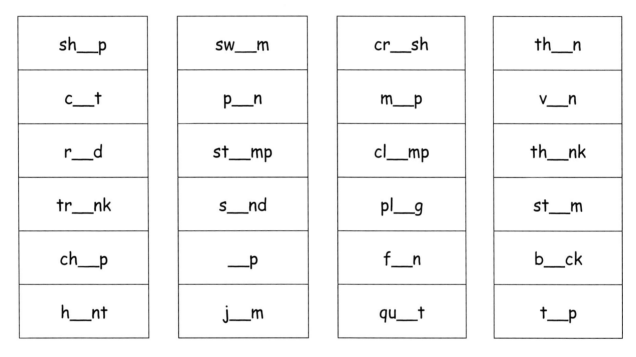

sh__p	sw__m	cr__sh	th__n
c__t	p__n	m__p	v__n
r__d	st__mp	cl__mp	th__nk
tr__nk	s__nd	pl__g	st__m
ch__p	__p	f__n	b__ck
h__nt	j__m	qu__t	t__p

Vowel dice template

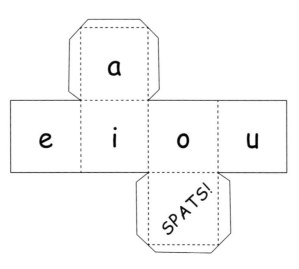

a

e   i   o   u

SPATS!

Worksheet C1

Preparation

- Cut up a copy of this sheet to produce the game cards – a selection of incomplete words (e.g. 'sh__p').

- Lay the game cards out on the table between the players.

- Provide each player with a coloured pen.

How to play SPATS

- Players take it in turns to throw the vowel dice, which has the word SPATS on one side and each of the five vowels on the other sides.

- If a player rolls a vowel they must attempt to make a word from the central assortment of game cards by adding the vowel in the space. If the player can create a word the vowel is written in and the game card is placed in front of that player. If no word can be created, play moves on to the next player.

- If a player rolls SPATS! the player's opponents must read out all the words on the game cards they have filled in. The player who rolled SPATS! then chooses a game card to steal from one of the opponents and that game card is placed face up in front of that player. If no opponents have any game cards, play moves on to the next player.

- Play ends when all the game cards have been transformed into words.

- The player with the most game cards (or the youngest in the event of a tie) throws the vowel dice to obtain the BONUS vowel.

- Words that have been created using the BONUS vowel are worth five points. All other words are worth one point. Players award themselves points for the words they have on the game cards in front of them at the end of play.

- The winner is the player with the highest number of points.

Worksheet D
Listening for Alice

Teaching advice

Primarily, listening skills are developed through this worksheet along with memory skills and, later, reading experience. By presenting the task as a game, a competitive element encourages the pupil to find ways of achieving success, developing focus and application.

Weak listening skills are often due to specific weaknesses within the audio modality, or through an overloading of the working memory if other decoding challenges are present. By reducing additional demands on the working memory (such as writing or reading), and by providing 'simple' replies to retain, audio memory skills are developed. Additional worksheets provide further practice, increasing the pupil's capabilities.

In class

Introduce the worksheet by reading through the introduction and examples together. Does the pupil understand the game? Play the game using questions 1–5, allowing you to judge the pupil's ability. According to ability, divide questions 1–20 into groups of questions and place the sheet in an envelope addressed to the reader. Retest ability during the next lesson by repeating familiar questions or by providing new ones.

Worksheet D
Listening for Alice

Adaptive possibilities

- Pupils can create their own questions (exercising writing and punctuation along with spelling).
- Use questions that relate to other curriculum material:

How many wives did Henry VIII have?
How many pennies are there in a pound?

- Introduce unfamiliar text alongside familiar words. When it is the pupil's turn to read, the sentences will be familiar, supporting their decoding skills.

Does a piranha have four legs?
What is the opposite of 'ceiling'?

- Intersperse simple questions with more complex ones:

What is your name?
What is a quarter of 16?
Are you a tiger?

- Develop audio discrimination with similar sounding words:

Can a spider ride a bike?
Is a baker's dozen thirty or thirteen loaves?

- Prepare short quizzes for pupils to read to each other.
- Experiment with different fonts for different readers.

Worksheet D1
Listening for Alice

Name:..

Date:.................................... Form:..........................

This worksheet requires two people.

On the back of this sheet is a list of questions. When a question is read out, give the answer to the PREVIOUS question!

Example

1. Do birds lay eggs?	SILENCE
2. How many days in the week?	'Yes'
3. Is the world flat?	'Seven'
4. How old are you?	'No'

Whenever a question includes the word 'Alice', the listener must put their hands on their head!

Example

1. Is it raining?	SILENCE
2. Is your name Alice?	(hands on head) 'Yes'/'No'
3. Where do tadpoles live?	'Yes'/'No'
4. What is the opposite of small?	'In water'
5. How many brothers do you have?	'Big'

Now play this at home. After you have been the listener, try out the game on someone else with you reading the questions.

This list of questions needs to be read out to a listener. When a question has been read out, the listener must give the answer to the PREVIOUS question (*see over for an example*).

1. How many days are there in a week?
2. What is the opposite of happy?
3. Is Alice a girl's name? (hands on head)
4. How many legs does a horse have?
5. What is three plus seven?

6. Which month follows August?
7. Are baby cats called kittens?
8. What is your name?
9. Which number follows 11?
10. Do camels lay eggs?

11. How many months are there in a year?
12. Does the word 'Alice' have five letters? (hands on head)
13. Which day follows Monday?
14. Are you a girl?
15. How many legs are there on a mouse?

16. Are you alive?
17. Is it snowing?
18. Which month follows May?
19. Does 'Alice' end with 'e'? (hands on head)
20. Am I older than you?

Worksheet E
Same Sound but Different Meaning

Teaching advice

Homophones frequently appear in the English language, causing a lot of confusion. The only way of ensuring success is by knowing the meaning of each word and then focusing in on its spelling. (Spelling traces are weaker for words whose meaning is not understood.)

Pupils with visual weaknesses are those most likely to make errors. Pupils with word-finding difficulties are also vulnerable to error as word meanings are often not established easily. Pupils with audio weaknesses are generally better at noticing the spelling differences between words such as 'knight' and 'night', but still need to have the meanings securely attached to each spelling.

In class

Read through the words together, identifying pairs, and creating meaningful sentences. Highlight spellings, attaching them to word meanings. Play Bingo by cutting up copies of the worksheet to make the components of the game. Players take it in turns to read out a word, followed by a meaningful sentence. Leave page 2 of the worksheet to be completed unrehearsed to measure the nature of need for further inputs. Provide similar Bingo games for holiday fun, or end-of-term amusement.

Worksheet E
Same Sound but Different Meaning

Adaptive possibilities

Playing Bingo is a fun way of overlearning lesson material and can be used to practise a variety of skills such as visual discrimination, visual memory, word meanings and usage.

- Use Bingo cards to identify between different groups:

living things : non-living things

verbs : nouns

- Use cards that contain similar sounding words to develop audio discrimination:

accept : except

tried : tired

- Practise the use of the apostrophe by presenting a key sentence containing a spelling on one of the Bingo cards:

He stepped in the cat's dinner.   cat's

The cats keep well away from our terrier.   cats

If players correctly match the word on their card with the correct spelling, a counter is placed on that word.

- Present pictures that have to be matched with words:

 physical
touch

 spoken
communication

Worksheet E1
Same Sound but Different Meaning

Name:..

Date:.. Form:........................

Read through these words and put each one into a meaningful sentence. Draw lines to match the pairs.

A

road	their	sore
red	write	guessed
knight	poor	mane

B

there	pour	main
read	night	rode
guest	saw	right

A

two	four	know
would	mints	sew
witch	wear	won

B

so	wood	mince
which	to	where
no	one	for

Choose the right word to fill in the following spaces:

1. He (saw/sore) .... (their/there) .... car driving along the (mane/main) .... (rode/road) ....

2. (There/Their) .... dog was lost in the (wood/would) .... all (night/knight) ....

3. The (night/knight) .... (road/rode) .... his horse through the dark (would/wood) .... to (wear/where) .... the (which/witch) .... was hiding.

4. I do not (no/know) .... how to (sew/so) .... on a button, but I'm (shore/sure) .... I could learn.

5. I ate (sew/so) .... many (mince/mints) .... my tongue got (saw/sore) ....

6. (There/Their) .... are only (four/for) .... days left of our holiday. I never want (to/too) .... leave.

7. He (guest/guessed) .... the closest (wait/weight) ...., and (one/won) ....the cake.

8. When I looked (through/threw) .... the keyhole and saw a rat wearing a hat, I hoped I was dreaming.

Worksheet F
Quiz Time!

Teaching advice

A quiz contains short reading exercises that cover a wide variety of topics. Quizzes make excellent tools for overlearning material as well as introducing new vocabulary and variety of expression. After sharing an initial investigation of the quiz's text the pupil completes the worksheet unaided, reinforcing reading skills and providing diagnostic details of their spelling and penmanship abilities through the provision of answers.

Quizzes can be easily tailored to meet individual need. Reading comprehension, sequencing weaknesses, decision-making and decoding accuracy can be practised along with answers that reiterate a spelling pattern, new terminology or mental calculation.

Examples

1. What is the last letter of alphabet?   (t) *Read carefully!*
3. Which month follows August?   *Sequencing, spelling*
4. Are nocturnal animals awake at night?   *Introducing 'nocturnal'*
13. If not, would you like one?   *Novel question format*
14. How high is a shed that stands beside a 3-metre tall tree that is twice the height of the shed?   *Draw picture to support decoding*
16. How many legs does a tortoise have?   *Reinforcing 'tortoise'*
17. Which month follows October?   *Repetition of sequence*
18. What colour are lemons?   *Checking spelling ability*

Worksheet F
Quiz Time!

Adaptive possibilities

- Use of repetitive language to establish new vocabulary:

  Are cats extinct?
  Are dinosaurs extinct?

- Overlearn topic material from other topics:

  Quelle heure est-il?
  Is a frog a mammal?
  How many legs do three ants have?

- Use quizzes to monitor level of reading comprehension.

  Are cows found in rural or urban areas?
  Change the vowel in 'post' to make something annoying.

- Overlearn spelling lessons through use of answers:

  Which season follows spring?   (double 'm')
  What is a baby sheep called?   (-mb ending)

- Encourage pupils to create questions from answers. They often find this harder than we expect, but it is a novel and challenging angle of approach that exercises the mind's way of connecting information.

  Answer: Paris   Question: ....
  Answer: Sometimes   Question: ....

- Pupils can write quizzes for others, exercising written (or word processing) skills, spelling, and ability to create a varied list of short questions.

A booklet of quizzes is useful holiday-work. Repetition of a familiar quiz or familiar questions helps to develop processing speed.

Worksheet F1
Quiz Time!

Name:..

Date:............................. Form:..................

1. What is the last letter of alphabet? ....

2. Which day follows yesterday? ....

3. Which month follows August? ....

4. Are nocturnal animals awake at night? ....

5. Do you like strawberries? ....

6. In which season does August fall? ....

7. What is the opposite of 'below'? ....

8. What is the opposite of 'angry'? ....

9. What is the plural of 'baby'? ....

10. Which month follows July? ....

11. How old are you? ....

12. Do you have a cat? ....

13. If not, would you like one? ....

14. How high is a shed that stands beside a 3-metre tall tree that is twice the height of the shed? ....

15. Do cabbages grow on trees? ....

16. How many legs does a tortoise have? ....

17. Which month follows October? ....

18. What colour are lemons? ....

19. Are you kind? ....

20. Which day comes before the day after yesterday? ....

21. Have you nearly finished? ....

22. Are you glad its nearly over? ....

23. Is this the final question? ....

Worksheet G
Opposite Sentences

Teaching advice

This worksheet provides the opportunity to discuss and develop the reading, spelling and expression of language.

Each sentence can be altered in a number of ways. This provides the opportunity for decision-making and variety of expression, which is good experience for many pupils. The resulting sentence must deliver an opposite meaning, not just a different one.

Example

'They started fighting at noon' could become:

> 'They stopped fighting at noon'
> or   'They started fighting at midnight'
> or   'Fighting ceased at noon.'
> or   'Peace was declared at midday'.

In class

Read through each sentence, developing decoding skills. Ensure that meanings are understood. Discuss possible alternatives, allowing the pupil to decide to what degree a sentence is changed (decision-making). Encourage copying skills when new sentences retain original words. Make use of the instruction to create sentences: what is a sentence, and how are speech marks and other punctuation used?

By discussing possible answers, rather than writing them down, audio memory skills are developed as the pupil retains ideas for use when completing the worksheet at a later time. Spelling inputs can be delivered alongside the worksheet (e.g. 'peace' using wooden letters), which are then reinforced through application.

Worksheet G
Opposite Sentences

Adaptive possibilities

- Integration of previously covered material:

  - remembering spelling patterns;
  - overlearning reading vocabulary;
  - using punctuation, e.g. apostrophes, question marks;
  - using 'dis-', 'mis-' and 'un-' to create opposites.

- Inclusion of names to develop phonic decoding:

  Mr Braintree …
  Adam Underfellow …
  Drippy Dewdrop …

- Include topic material covered elsewhere on the curriculum.

  Cleopatra was born in 69BC   (Cleopatra died in 30BC)
  Rabbits are living things   (Rocks are non-living things)
  Il fait beau temps   (Il fait mauvais temps)

- Differentiation:

  - Supply opposite sentences with spaces for key words for pupil with penmanship and/or word-finding difficulties.
  - Read sentences aloud (no visual application) to pupils with weaknesses in audio modality to develop listening skills (this requires a scribe or an audio recording machine).

- Extend the level of complexity:

  My aunt is my mother's sister   (My uncle is my father's brother)

Worksheet G1
Opposite Sentences

Name:..

Date:.............................. Form:.......................

Write a sentence that means the **opposite** to the one shown.

1. My granny does not like loud noises.

   ....

2. They started fighting at noon.

   ....

3. I closed the back door.

   ....

4. Yesterday, John slowly paddled up the river because he had plenty of time on his hands.

   ....

5. What an ugly baby!

   ....

6. Yesterday, I bought a new white shirt.

   ....

7. He dropped his piece of cake on the floor.

....

8. Katherine sat on the step and cried.

....

9. 'Time for bed', said Mum.

....

10. She covered the parrot's cage with a cloth.

....

11. 'Can you turn the music off?' asked Mr Brown.

....

12. A little trickle of water came out of the tap.

....

13. This is not the final sentence.

....

Worksheet H
Looks Like...

Teaching advice

For pupils with visual discrimination weaknesses, words such as 'quiet' and 'quite', 'then' and 'when' are often confused. This worksheet helps them to see why they make these errors, and helps to develop proofreading skills. Visual discrimination weaknesses also predispose a reading style dependent on contextual and initial lettering guesswork. The second side of the worksheet develops those skills and provides initial blends for investigation.

In class

Read the introduction together. Read through the words in the box, providing a meaningful sentence for each word. Leave the questions for the pupil to complete on their own. Read through the second side of worksheet, letting the pupil verbalise answers (discussing spellings if necessary) and noting their ability to provide appropriate suggestions. Look through the initial blends, reinforcing the input by using wooden letters to create familiar words sharing these blends. Note the blends the pupil finds difficult and provide variations of this sheet to practise others.

The pupil should then complete the worksheet, unaided if possible, before the next lesson, when it can be reviewed.

Worksheet H
Looks Like...

Adaptive possibilities

- As with many worksheets, reading experience is delivered at a level achievable through the shared introduction to the text. Use this factor to introduce new terminology:

  Looks like 'muscle' but is a type of shellfish.
  Looks like 'entire' but means to lure away.

- Introduce new reading (and spelling) vocabulary:

  Looks like 'tried' but means very sleepy.
  Looks like 'dessert' but is a large expanse of sand.

- Use words misread (and misspelled) elsewhere:

  Looks like 'dark' but is the sound made by a dog.
  Looks like 'hoping' but means jumping on one foot.

- Use different coloured paper. This can reduce the disorderly appearance of words for pupils who find that letters 'swim about' when black letters are presented on bright white paper.
- Ask a variety of questions, some with a single answer, others with possibilities to choose from:

  A snake is a reptile. A hamster is a m ....
  The boy found a s .... on the doorstep.

- Adapt the worksheet to include middle and ending letters too.

Worksheet H1
Looks Like...

Name:...
Date:.................................... Form:...........................

Some words are easily mistaken for other, similar words, e.g. 'through' and 'thought'. Read the following words and then answer the questions:

bought	brought	strip	stripe
place	places	through	thought
quiet	quite	spirit	sprite
shoulder	shudder	what	that

1. It looks like 'quite' but means the opposite of noisy.

   ....

2. It looks like 'brought' but means to have paid money for something.

   ....

3. It looks like 'shudder' but is at the top of your arm.

   ....

4. It looks like 'through' but is an idea that passes through your head.

   ....

5. It looks like 'strip' but is a line of colour.

   ....

Worksheet H1
Page 2

Complete these sentences:

1. The boy's name is S ....
2. The day after T .... is W ....
3. My favourite colour is b ....
4. Yesterday, the elephant was given a b ....
5. We like to play t ....
6. I b .... my hamster into school.

Complete the following words however you choose:

bl ....   spr ....   tr ....

gl ....   shr ....   ex ....

Kn ....   thr ....   wr ....

fl ....   all ....   dis ....

br ....   ph ....   acc ....

Worksheet I
Aesop's Fables

Teaching advice

Fables are very useful stories to use for reading comprehension, memory and writing development. The stories are short and meaningful and carry messages that can be discussed and related to everyday life.

In class

Begin by reading the story of how the sun and the wind compete to be the one to remove the traveller's coat. By reading together, reading decoding weaknesses are supported, and then reinforced by the pupil reading the story again unaided. Repetitive language, shortness of passages and an active storyline all encourage the pupil to achieve success. The task of creating a cartoon develops sequencing skills, artistic ability and transference of written meaning into pictorial displays. Dyslexic pupils are often artistic so enjoy the chance to demonstrate these skills. Those with penmanship weaknesses are also aided by the pictorial challenge, particularly as the boxes provided are (intentionally) small to encourage careful application.

The second side of the worksheet provides exercises that practise reading, memory and drawing skills. Discussing the value of maxims also develops conversational skills.

Worksheet I
Aesop's Fables

Adaptive possibilities

- Fables can be used to practise audio memory skills:

  - have the pupil listen to the story then repeat it;
  - have the pupil listen to the story then write it.

- Fables can be used to practise reading comprehension:

  - have the pupil read the story then answer questions;
  - follow a reading of the fable with a discussion of its possible message; key words are clarity, effectiveness and relevance;
  - present the fable using the original phraseology and then translate it into modern language.

- Fables can be used to practise written compositions:

  - have the pupil read the story then write their own version.

- Fables can be used to analyse structure of written essays:

  - present the fable without punctuation for correction;
  - identify and compare beginnings, middles and endings.

- Fables can be used for spelling practice:

  - present the fable with blanks in place of chosen words.

Worksheet I1
Aesop's Fables

Name:..
Date:.. Form:.........................

A fable is a story. It tells of events in a way that demonstrates a message to the reader. Read this story then draw four pictures to illustrate the story as a cartoon.

ONE OF AESOP'S FABLES

One day, the North Wind and the Sun were having an argument. Each claimed that he was stronger than the other. At last they agreed to try their powers against a traveller to see which of them could strip him of his cloak.

   The North Wind went first. He blew and blew with all his might trying to strip the traveller of his cloak. The traveller bent his head against the wind and pulled his cloak tighter around his body. The harder the wind blew, the tighter the man held on to his cloak.

   Then it was the Sun's turn. As he shone down, the warmth of his rays fell gently on to the traveller, who soon released the grip on his cloak. As the Sun shone warmer, the traveller took off his cloak, and happily flung it over his shoulder and continued on his way.

Persuasion is often more effective than force.

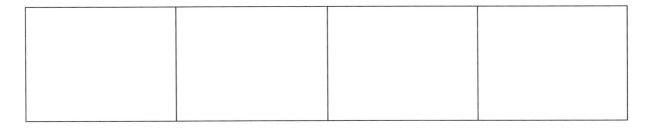

Here is another of Aesop's fables. Read it through and learn the story well enough to tell the story from memory.

A young boy put his hand into a sweet jar and grasped as many toffee twists as he could. But when he tried to pull it out again, he found he couldn't do so because the neck of the jar was too small for such a handful. Unwilling to lose his sweets but unable to withdraw his hand, the boy burst into tears.

'Come, my dear boy, don't be so greedy', said a bystander who saw where the trouble lay. 'Be content with half the amount, and you'll be able to get your hand out without difficulty.'

Do not attempt too much at once.

A thirsty crow came upon a pitcher with some water in it, but so little was there that, try as she might, she could not reach it with her beak.

At first, she thought of knocking the pitcher over, spilling the precious liquid on to the earth. But she knew that the water would seep away, leaving only a dribble for her thirst. So she hopped about the pitcher, eying the challenge before her. At last she hit upon a clever plan.

Espying some small pebbles on the ground around her, she carefully transferred them into the pitcher, filling it with stones until the water level had risen to a height within her reach. What a clever bird !

Patience will succeed.

Draw a picture of the crow considering the problem before her.

Worksheet J
Letter Groups

Adaptive possibilities

- **Play games**
  A number of games practise the creation of words from component letter groups. Tailor-make your own or/and find them in catalogues and shops. Games such as these can provide 'wet-play' entertainment as well as in-class learning. (Note the effect of regional accents when using commercially produced games.)

- **Use the worksheets to support other languages**
  By breaking down foreign words into their component sounds, the pupil becomes practised at identifying unfamiliar letter group displays and pronunciation, e.g. 'le ch-ou', 'je jou-e'.

- **Identify root words**
  Use words such as 'un-trust-worthy', breaking the words into chunks of meaning rather than sound. Encourage pupils to recognise both meaning and sounds within words.

- **Focus on letter rules**
  Investigate the construction of words such as 'ac-cept' and 'gu-ide', to highlight the variations of 'c' and 'g'. Words such as 'excite-ment', 'excit-ing' and 'excitedly', support lessons on vowels, and explain why the final 'e' is retained before '-ment' but not '-ing'. Dyslexic pupils need to understand rules in order to successfully apply them.

- **(Mis)pronouncing irregular spellings to remember them**
  Think about words such as friend ('fri-end') and important ('im-port-ANT').

Worksheet J1
Letter Groups

Name:..

Date:.. Form:...........................

Words can be broken down into chunks of sound, e.g. sh-op.
Connect the following sound chunks to make three words:

mis	may
dis	tie
un	take

Which word means the same as 'error'? ....

Draw lines between the following chunks of sound to make four
words, then make three new words of your own:

shr	ink	shr ....
spr	out	spr ....
str	ing	str ....

Which word means the opposite of 'grow bigger'? ....

Read through the following letter groups:

ex	pec	ta	tion
ex	plan	a	tion

Write a word beside each picture, breaking up each spelling into chunks of sound.

....

....

Replace the underlined section of the following words with your choice of letter group presented in brackets:

in<u>vi</u>tation   [fes/den]   ....

<u>con</u>struction   [des/in]   ....

explo<u>sion</u>   [ding/ded]   ....

Write down the answers to the following questions:

1. Which month follows August? ....

2. What is the name of the boy who owns Pooh Bear?
   ....

3. To let people know about our party, we need to send them an ....

Worksheet K
Listening for Sound

Teaching advice

Memory weaknesses often reduce the ability of dyslexic pupils to retain material within their working memory long enough for it to be processed effectively. Inputs delivered via speech are frequently forgotten by pupils with audio memory weaknesses, and similar sounding words can be confused through weak audio discrimination skills.

This worksheet delivers exercises that focus on sounds within words, and whole-word retention. By developing pupils' responses with progressive worksheets, the skills of audio processing can be enhanced and progress monitored.

In class

Explain the first exercise and complete it in class, reading sounds 1–7 to the pupil. Tick the answer (providing a reassuring movement for the pupil) and praise their work, whatever the achieved level of performance.

Introduce the game on the second side as a fun challenge, making up some examples to illustrate the nature of the game. Place the sheet in a sealed envelope for parents to deliver at home.

The home activity puts your ears to the test by the pupil!

Worksheet K
Listening for Sound

Adaptive possibilities

- **Extending the audio memory challenge**
  - Present longer batches of key words to choose from.
  - Ask more complex questions.

- **Incorporating numeracy**

one/nine/thirty-two	Which is an even number?
six/three/two	Put these numbers into one sum.

- **Overlearning other subjects**

Henry VI/Henry VIII/Henry I:	Who had six wives?
Hadrian/Boadicea/Centurion:	Spell one of them.
huit/une/quatre:	Write these down in a sum.
Mercury/Pluto/Earth:	Which is nearest the sun?

- **Writing exercises**
  - The pupil writes down answers instead of saying them.
  - The pupil creates an ear-test for others. (Discuss variability of questions and key words.)
  - Using word processing skills, the pupil creates a test in print form.

- **Visual memory exercises**
  - Key words are shown to the pupil, then removed from sight while the question is read and answered.
  - Pupils are shown a whole set of words or pictures before a whole set of questions is delivered.

Worksheet K1
Listening for Sound

Exercises delivered by adults to monitor listening skills

Name:..

Date:.. Form:..........................

This worksheet practises the skills of focused hearing, identification and memory. Follow the instructions, noting the pupil's ability in these different areas. Speak clearly.

If you suspect lip-reading is aiding the pupil's reply, stand behind them. Practise sounds that cause initial errors.

Provide the pupil with the initial sound (words in italics are for clarification only, and not for reading aloud). Ask the pupil to identify which of the words that follow contain that sound.

1.   'sp'   (*as in 'spot'*)   [lost/wasp]
2.   'ip'   (*as in 'sip'*)   [strips/stripe]
3.   'gr'   (*as in 'grid'*)   [ground/drowned]
4.   'thr'   (*as in 'three'*)   [freesia/thresher]
5.   'imp'   (*as in 'limp'*)   [implore/employ]
6.   'a'   (*as in 'pat'*)   [artist/artisan]
7.   'pl'   (*as in 'play'*)   [blade/played]

If the audio memory is weak, errors can occur because the pupil is unable to remember which sound they are listening for. If audio discrimination is weak, pupil may confuse similar sounds such as 'pl' and 'bl', 'ar' and 'dr'.

A QUIZ FOR THE EARS

This game requires a player to retain three words in their audio memory before choosing one of them to answer a question.

  Read out the three words on the left, then ask the question. Tick the answer presented. The questions appear in different forms, some more complex than others. Extend sheets according to need and ability.

1. game/gale/gate   Something you play
2. please/freeze/knees   The word that starts with 'k'
3. cat/cabbage/cardigan   A non-living thing
4. four/two/hedgehog   Use the words in one sentence
5. red/orange/green   The one containing the most 'e's
6. pink/yellow/brown   The colour of flushed cheeks

1. lightning/lighten/lightening   The opposite of 'darken'
2. England/America/France   Which is the biggest?
3. May/June/July   Which month comes next?
4. June/July/August   Make a sentence with each word
5. photosynthesis/centigrade/problematical   What were the three words presented in the last question?
6. grovel/gravel/drivel   The last word, alphabetically

Extra activity

Create an ear quiz for your teacher using six questions.

Worksheet L
Every Picture Tells a Story

Teaching advice

The construction of structured, informative and descriptive writing is difficult for many dyslexics to achieve. Apart from spelling demands (which should be relegated to the proofreading stage so as not to restrict word usage and confidence), the working memory has to integrate penmanship, word association, sequential ordering and grammar. Many pupils also lack the ability to perceive the reader's needs and will consequently fail to include all necessary information.

Through asking questions, the mind collates associated words and becomes more skilled at recognising details exhibited in pictorial displays.

In class

Having considered the questions provided, request a verbal descriptive passage to accompany each picture. Focus on the appearance of full stops and commas (where the speaker pauses), if necessary reduce use of the word 'it' (e.g. 'It is a house' becomes 'This is a picture of a house'), and discuss where different pictures might appear, and for what purpose, and then leave written completion for homework.

Worksheet L
Every Picture Tells a Story

Adaptive possibilities

- **Use pictures that contain implication**
  For example, for a picture showing a child crying beside a broken window, note the ability of the pupil to consider different possibilities:
  - the child broke the window and is fearful of the consequences;
  - the child was beside the window when it was broken;
  - the child is crying with cold in a house with broken windows.

- **Support second languages**
  - Repeat familiar pictures and provide key vocabulary.

- **Use diagrams and charts that display information**
  Examples are graphs, family trees, pie charts and timetables.

- **Support mainstream curriculum topics**
  - Provide pictures associated with geography (e.g. the aftermath of an earthquake), history (e.g. a medieval house), science (e.g. a microscope) and so on, that reinforce study of these topics elsewhere.

- **Write descriptions that require pictures**

Worksheet L1
Every Picture Tells a Story

Name:...
Date:... Form:.........................

Examine these pictures then write a story or explanation to match each one. To help you provide lots of details, ask yourself 'why?', 'where?', 'what?', 'who?' and 'when?' to prompt ideas.

Example

Why is there a kangaroo?
Where are the people who live here?
What is the building made of?
Who lives nearby?
When are these events happening?

Example

Why were these buildings built?
Where could these buildings be?
What is the surrounding land like?
Who lives in the house?
When were the buildings built?

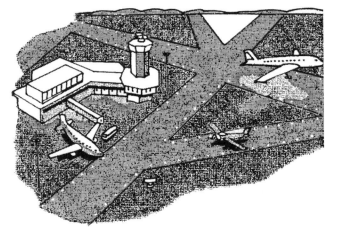

Example

Why is there more than one runway?
Where might this airport be?
What is the tall tower for?
Who might be due to arrive?
When would weather affect flights?

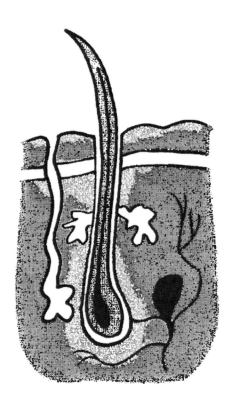

Example

Why do we need to label this diagram?
Where is the skin's surface?
What is a hair follicle?
Who needs to know this information?
When would this diagram be used?

Worksheet M
Changing Root Words

Adaptive possibilities

- **Integrate individual errors**
  Worksheets covering words that are frequently misspelled by individual pupils can be easily created and used for assessment purposes as well as teaching.

- **Support second languages**
  Pupils who find the identification of word components difficult in English will meet similar difficulties in other languages. Use colour to highlight unfamiliar letter-to-sound groups (e.g. verb endings). Ensure that word meanings are fully understood, perhaps requesting a drawing to accompany each word to support learning.

- **Focus on specific spelling rules**
  Create worksheets that include words that are similar in nature, to result in repetitive application of a spelling rule.

- **Use sheets to monitor learning**
  Following the introduction of a spelling rule, or individual spelling application, present the worksheet without much introduction in order to access the level of memory traces.

Worksheet M1
Changing Root Words

Name:...
Date:... Form:...........................

Change the following words by adding letters at the beginning or end of the root word. Write the new words in the boxes. Then choose one of the words you have made, cover the box of words, and write down a meaningful sentence.

1. clip

....

2. play

....

3. surprise

4. prepare

5. cry

Worksheet N
Finding Connections

Teaching advice

Word comprehension and word-finding difficulties are often caused by a weakness in associating connected words. For example, when reading, writing or hearing the word 'doctor', words such as 'injury', 'hospital' and 'patient' are known to become primed by centres in the brain associated with semantic storage. Within the dyslexic profile, a lack of this priming is frequently seen to occur, hampering fluency of reading, writing and speech. Exercises that develop this skill are therefore valuable, and ones that similarly exercise the association between different numbers (worksheet page 2) support the recognition of numerical connections.

In class

Read through the words, ensuring that their meanings are understood. Discuss spellings, particularly when oddities are present, e.g. 'ocean' and 'niece'. These sheets are designed to be achievable; they provide single-word reading experience and the opportunity to include spelling lessons along with the underlying task of associating words through meaning. The numerical exercises also act as familiarisation exercises. Frequent presentation of number associations helps to establish stronger memory traces and connective recognition.

Worksheet N
Finding Connections

Adaptive possibilities

- **Support spelling patterns**
  By collecting words that share a spelling pattern unfamiliar words can be introduced into the reading and spelling vocabulary (e.g. 'dumb', 'thumb', 'crumb' and 'lamb').

- **Support identification of homophones**
  Words such as 'site'/'sight', 'poll'/'pole', 'mince'/'mints' can be included. The pupil has then to determine which to choose when required to encircle words connected by meaning.

site/sight	word associated with senses
poll/pole	word associated with voting
mince/mints	word associated with butcher

- **Use the worksheet to prepare for written work**
  Delivering one of these worksheets prior to a written exercise (e.g. Write a passage entitled 'Life on the Ocean Waves'), introduces and familiarises pupils with vocabulary that will prompt ideas, add expression to their writing and support spelling weaknesses.

Worksheet N1
Finding Connections

Name:..

Date:.. Form:.........................

Read through the following words:

stone	cloak	coast	roast	crab
cabbage	plank	climb	oak	friend
earwig	flyer	view	fountain	wave
boat	fisherman	drip	limb	dumb
niece	elephant	trout	road	tide
boast	moan	ocean	swimmer	toad
voice	surf	lifeboat	swamp	coat
oasis	goat	note	angler	yacht
ocean	gloating	dingy	bloater	hutch

1. Underline the words that share an 'oa' spelling pattern.

2. Draw a ring round the words whose meaning is connected with water.

Read through the following numbers:

38	42	50	13	14
15	77	140	500	45
21	42	56	57	95
63	65	701	605	35

1. Underline the numbers that can be exactly divided by 7.
2. Draw a ring round the numbers that can be exactly divided by 5.

Read through the following numbers:

40	50	60	70	80
32	470	78	49	500
1008	30	45	46	96
42	63	3002	55	860

1. Underline the numbers that can be exactly divided by 2.
2. Draw a ring round the numbers that can be exactly divided by 10.

Worksheet O
Written Expression

Teaching advice

Most dyslexic pupils find the production of written work difficult. Memory weaknesses reduce the capacity to manipulate thoughts, penmanship, expression and spelling simultaneously, requiring preparation techniques to collate ideas before the construction of written passages begins. Support is also needed in creating written work that involves specific styles of delivery, language and punctuation.

In class

Introduce the terms 'fiction' and 'non-fiction', supporting them with examples of each. Discuss a possible non-fictional storyline and allow the pupil to write key words and phrases in the boxes provided. It is often useful to begin with the story's middle (where the action takes place) enabling the characters, timing and place required for the beginning to be matched accordingly, followed by the ending (the resolution of the drama). The pupil writes up the story and the fictional passages for homework, by hand, unless the use of word-processing skills is more appropriate. Performance results identify features that require additional input.

Worksheet O
Written Expression

Adaptive possibilities

- **Change formats**
  You could introduce changes in narrative passages, sentence lengths (affecting pace and emotion), paragraphs, variety of expression, characterisation and different genres of writing.

- **Use different planning techniques**
  Examples might include 'spider diagrams' and mind mapping, pictorial sketches and word prompts (e.g. 'why?', 'where?', 'when?', 'who?' and 'what?').

- **Incorporate mainstream topics**

  'What is a volcano?'

  'Describe one of your friends in French.'

- **Focus on the brevity of planning**
  - Encourage the application of *brief* phrases and single words when creating planning notes.
  - Present stories that the pupil reduces into notes.
  - Provide key words for inclusion in factual passages.

Worksheet 01
Written Expression

Name:..
Date:.. Form:...........................

Planning a FICTIONAL piece of writing

1. A goldfish has an adventure. What happens?

beginning	
middle	
ending	

2. Write up your story.

Title: ……………………………………

Writing FACTUAL accounts

1. What is a coin?

2. What is a dandelion?

3. What is ugliness?

4. Describe one of your friends.

Worksheet P
Number Work

Teaching advice

Word-association difficulties are often found in the dyslexic profile, resulting in a lack of speaking, reading and writing fluidity. A similar difficulty in recognising patterns and associations between numbers affects the learning of tables and manipulation of numbers. If the relationships between numbers such as '12', '4' and '16' are not recognised, progress is greatly reduced.

In class

Using materials to emphasise number size and the coded display of numbers (107 is a coded display reliant on position and clarity of penmanship), investigate possible relationships between the batches of numbers displayed on the first page of the worksheet. Many of the numbers presented contain more than one pattern of association that can be threaded across the page. Discuss connections and leave the pupil to complete the exercise for homework.

Page 2 of this worksheet develops audio memory and the manipulation of different types of information presented verbally. An introductory review is not required but adult participation is necessary for completion of the tasks. The pupil's responses can be written on the sheet, providing details of achievement level.

Worksheet P
Number Work

Adaptive possibilities

- **Vary the way numbers are displayed**
  Use fractions, decimals, large and small numbers, Roman numerals and written words (e.g. 'seventy-one').

- **Overlearn table knowledge**
  Support the development of multiplication and division through the extensive coverage of numbers to increase familiarity of recognising connections.

	14	28	35	7000
7	70	56	112	224
	28	700	7000	42

- **Vary visual presentation**
  Use coloured paper, or larger and smaller font sizes, and note any effect on a pupil's ability to identify connections.

- **Develop mental arithmetic**
  By varying the nature of the material on page 2 of the worksheet, achievable mental arithmetic exercises (7 + 3 =) can be extended (7 + 3 + 3 =) to develop memory capacity and skills.

Worksheet P1
Number Work

Name:..

Date:.................................... Form:........................

Start with the single number then look across the page to see if there is a route you could take that joins the numbers. Join the numbers with a line. Write down the connection.

```
        5     2     9     0     1
  4     8     3     7    10     6
        1     6     6     8     9
```

One number line: add one to each number
....

```
        1     2    32    10    52
  2    12     6    42    11    12
        4    22     8    42     2
```

....

```
       22    11    40     9     8
 13    12    39    10    65    78
       26    31    52    49    58
```

....

© 2015, *Supporting Key Stage 2 and 3 Dyslexic Pupils, their Teachers and Support Staff: The Dragonfly Worksheets, 2nd edition*, Sally Raymond, Routledge.

Read the following passages aloud to the pupil. Repeat *the whole* passage if requested or necessary.

1. The tallest boy is standing beside the shortest girl. The shortest boy is also next to the tallest boy.

   How many people are there altogether?

   Describe how they are standing in a line.

2. On Friday, 10-year-old John is going swimming with three of his friends. One friend arrives with her older brother who wants to swim too. Another friend forgets her towel. Another friend goes to the wrong swimming pool, so he never turns up.

   How many people are in John's group?

   How many of them are girls and how many are boys?

   The girl without a towel goes swimming. How might she get dried afterwards?

   On which day of the week does all this happen?

3. Oh what a drag, I've come to school without my bag.
   Oh what a pain, I've travelled to France instead of ....
   Oh what a shame, the racehorse is ....
   Oh what a pity, I'm lost in the ....
   Oh what a bore, he's locked the front ....
   Oh what a joke, the can's empty of ....
   Oh what a surprise, the mice have blue ....
   Oh what a mess she has spilled down her ....

Worksheet Q
The Language of Mathematics

Teaching advice

This worksheet develops reading skills, the translation of written sentences into sums, the understanding of specific terms and the following of written instructions.

Dyslexic pupils often find it difficult to identify the nature of a numerical operation required to solve a problem swathed in written language. They may choose an 'inefficient' approach (e.g. addition in place of multiplication) and need the discovery of experience to identify relationships between different mathematical operations developing flexibility of thought.

In class

Support reading skills and discuss word meanings and spellings of unfamiliar text. Investigate the possible approaches required to achieve success, encouraging the display of workings and checking of answers. Answers also need to be appropriately completed ('30 legs' not '30'). Ensure that a ruler, compass and so on are available and leave completion of the worksheet for homework. Analysis of performance allows further worksheets to be developed enhancing areas of weakness and extending areas of ability.

Worksheet Q
The Language of Mathematics

Adaptive possibilities

- **Extend existing knowledge**
  Using number knowledge such as 3 + 7 =10, include tasks that call upon 30 + 70, 0.3 + 0.7, 100 − 70, 233 + 767, etc.

- **Use large numbers**
  Once mathematical operations have been introduced, utilise large numbers for addition, subtraction, multiplication and division. It is very rewarding for a pupil to realise that once the display and sequential aspects are followed they can achieve impressive calculations. Large numbers can be initially daunting; familiarity reduces intimidation.

- **Introduce complex statements carefully**
  Dyslexic pupils often find the transposing of words into mathematical equations difficult. Use simple sentences first, repeating them with additional information and/or additional computational demands:

  How many days are there in three weeks?

  If John goes on holiday for three weeks and spends £1.50 a day, how much will he spend?

Worksheet Q1
The Language of Mathematics

Name:..

Date:... Form:..........................

1. How many legs do six mice have? ....

2. If there are six sweets in a jar and you eat one-third of the sweets, how many are left? ....

3. How many legs do sixty mice have? ....

4. A can of coke costs 60p from a machine or 45p from a shop. What is the difference between the two prices? ....

5. How many legs do 36 mice have? ....

6. What is 50% of 40? ....

7. If you receive a 10th of 60, what will you get? ....

8. What is 50% of 200? ....

9. If five people buy four pizzas and share the cost, how much will each person pay if the pizzas cost £2.50 each? ....

10. How many legs do four spiders have? ....

11. If it is 3.35am now, what will the time be in 15 minutes? ....

12. Continue this pattern:
    3   30   6   60   9   ....

13 Write down three prime numbers: ....

14. Write down an addition sum:

....

15. Write down a multiplication sum:

....

16. Draw a triangle:

17. Draw a circle using a compass:

18. Draw a rectangle. Draw horizontal lines to divide it into sixths:

Worksheet R
Speedy Decisions

Teaching advice

This worksheet develops processing speed. As sheet material becomes familiar, pupils achieve more rapid reading, comprehension and applicational skills.

In class

Provide three duplicates of the worksheet labelled A, B and C. Support reading skills and comprehension of the task. After reviewing the material, allow the pupil to complete the first copy of the worksheet in class, noting the time required for completion. The remaining worksheets are completed for homework; the pupil noting down the times of commencement and completion in order to calculate their speed of application.

On page 2 of the worksheet, tasks include an anagram box (write words created from 'acres' around the box), a vertical rather than horizontal display (parts of speech) and a choice of answers (both oxygen and mercury are elements, but only mercury is a liquid at room temperature).

Note too the variety of symbolic displays used in this worksheet: words, letters, numbers, % sign, etc. When creating further worksheets, incorporate additional displays to establish understanding and familiarity.

Worksheet R
Speedy Decisions

Adaptive possibilities

- **Use a variety of displays**
  Once the nature of the worksheet has been established, incorporate a variety of displays: horizontal and vertical columns, scattered words that need pairing, words that have more than one match, etc.

- **Deliver worksheets that require written application**
  Instead of reading and matching words, provide only one list of words that the pupil must read and then write in an appropriate match:

  season   ....

  mammal   ....

  film star   ....

  As this worksheet is initially completed in class, the prompting of suggestions and spellings can be provided. Whether the pupil duplicates identical answers on subsequent sheets, or variations, is left to the pupil and teacher to decide (according to ability and need).

- **Repeat identical sheets at a later date and compare completion times with initial applications**

Worksheet R1
Speedy Decisions

Name:..

Date:... Form:.........................

This sheet has been duplicated three times. Each time you complete a sheet, try to do so faster than you did last time!

a fish	Sheffield Wednesday
a colour	envy
6 × 6	thirty
a piece of furniture	thirty-six
day of the week	rabbit
month following August	trout
a mammal	purple
an emotion	July
5 × 6	Wednesday
a football team	sofa
a word starting with J	September

a group of people	Robin
a bird	Y
a season	uncle
month following November	crowd
a number less than twelve	eight
a relation	gloss
a group of lions	robin
a letter of the alphabet	December
a mathematical symbol	+
a boy's name	pride
a type of paint	Autumn

cedar	a fruit
violin	a reptile
metre	the site of a battle
swarm	4 × 6
litter	a measure of volume
24	a type of wood
pineapple	a musical instrument
Hastings	a group of bees
litre	rubbish
40	27 + 13
lizard	a measure of length

4 × 6	36
9 × 6	30
6 × 6	24
3 × 6	18
5 × 6	54

noun	adjective	verb
smelling	smell	smelly

carbon dioxide	liquid at room temperature
oxygen	element
mercury	separation technique
chromatography	compound

0.25	33%
75%	54
9 × 6	a quarter
a third	three-quarters

A	C	R
	E	S

Worksheet S
Plurals

Teaching advice

Creating the plural spellings of words involves the identification of endings requiring '-es', those that require 's', those that need additional changes (e.g. -f to –ves), and irregular forms (e.g. sheep/sheep, tooth/teeth).

Mainstream English lessons cover this topic but dyslexic pupils frequently require additional inputs and revision before memory traces are established sufficiently to achieve success, particularly in free writing.

This worksheet is not designed to act as a teaching tool, but rather to provide revision, reinforcement and assessment of ability concerning a topic that is more appropriately introduced alongside a game (see adaptive possibilities), where a variety of plurals are experienced before different suffixing rules are introduced. Dyslexic pupils do not easily associate the word 'lady' with a 'y' ending due to spelling weaknesses. Attention also needs to be paid to the articulation of words (e.g. 'knives') to ensure that they are not using 'knifes' in their speech.

In class

Deliver this worksheet following introductory inputs. Appraisal of results indicates level of ability.

Worksheet S
Plurals

Adaptive possibilities

- **Support second languages**
  Focus on the changes in root words required when using foreign languages.

- **Use other types of word changes**

  Change these verbs from the past into present tense:

  he swam   ....   she slept   ....
  they drank   ....   it grew   ....

  Name the males that match these females:

  lioness   ....   vixen   ....
  Miss   ....   spinster   ....

  Write down the opposites to these words:

  ugly   ....   boiling   ....
  fresh   ....   winter   ....

  Change these adjectives into adverbs:

  brave   ....   mad   ....
  angry   ....   careful   ....

Worksheet S1
Plurals

Name:..
Date:.................................... Form:...........................

Write down the plural of the following words:

1. town ....   11. tomato ....
2. baby ....   12. cry ....
3. puppy ....   13. flurry ....
4. castle ....   14. mouse ....
5. trouble ....   15. pleasure ....
6. knife ....   16. disease ....
7. leaf ....   17. capsule ....
8. opposite ....   18. sympathy ....
9. enemy ....   19. symphony ....
10. kindness ....   20. similarity ....

Write down the term for a collection of the following:

1. bees ....   4. eggs ....
2. sheep ....   5. fish ....
3. sparrows ....   6. cut flowers ....

Write down the singular of the following words:

1. pennies   ....
2. flies   ....
3. wives   ....
4. teeth   ....
5. sheep   ....
6. potatoes   ....

7. marshes   ....
8. entries   ....
9. lives   ....
10. collections   ....
11. ruins   ....
12. deliveries   ....

Instead of writing a number, use a term that indicates quantity, for example:

a few   some   a pair   a flock   etc.

1. (12) .... children were in the class.

2. (2) .... blackbirds are nesting in that bush.

3. I found (5) .... sheep in our garden yesterday.

4. He has (342) .... different beer mats.

5. I have (1) .... PlayStation game.

6. There are (453,753) .... of stars visible in the sky.

Worksheet T
Adding an Interesting Ending

Teaching advice

This worksheet practises contextual reading and written application. A lack of reading ability reduces the variety of storylines, information and writing styles experienced, so short passages like this are very valuable. The pupil is required to not only read and comprehend the text, but also access implication. So often, an ability to decode words is taken as a measure of reading skill, but unless comprehension and implication are extracted too, the purpose and rewards of reading are not achieved.

In class

Read through the passage together. Some pupils will make increased errors when required to read aloud, so it is useful to provide them with the opportunity to read the passage silently before adding the output of speech. Test reading comprehension and implication by asking questions about the text. Discuss the actions of different characters, and the manner in which suspense and expectation are expressed. Discuss possible endings and leave the pupil to complete the story for homework by hand or using word processing skills. Read through the information on page 2 of the worksheet, discussing methods of planning as well as ideas for inclusion in their reply. Provide key-word spellings and review next lesson.

Worksheet T
Adding an Interesting Ending

Adaptive possibilities

- **Use the pupil's own work**
  Write a story based on a pupil's piece of creative writing, enabling them to see what additional or different approaches could be made. A new ending is then created.

- **Use different fonts, text size and coloured paper**
  Some pupils find different sizes and types of format easier to assimilate. Information gained from these exercises can then be used in the differentiation of other work. Different coloured texts (achievable by printing worksheets out on colour printers) and/or different coloured paper may reduce visual assimilation difficulties experienced by some pupils.

- **Reproduce factual pieces**
  When completing a factual text, fewer possibilities are available. The ending is usually presented as a summary of information and a conclusion, helping pupils to fashion the ending of passages that may, for example, compare or evaluate two or more issues. Mainstream curriculum material can be used or you could incorporate pupils' hobbies.

Worksheet T1
Adding an Interesting Ending

Name:..
Date:.. Form:...........................

Exercise 1

We arrived at the beach about 8am. Our four double canoes were lined up along the sand, their noses pointing eagerly out to sea. I pulled on a bright yellow life-jacket handed out by the Seasports rep. and tried to look calm, but it wasn't easy. Out there I could see cold pummelling waves and endless grey water. Was it safe? Was this fun? Looking around, I saw my friends were full of seaside madness: chasing around the boats; play-fighting with paddles; Mark being carried down to the water's edge for a dunking. Was I really the only one who felt scared? Did I dare find out?

By nine o'clock we had all the safety gear on and had been given the basic instructions. We weren't going far; just along the coast to a couple of bays, at the second of which a BBQ lunch would await us. I felt hungry already. John gave the signal, then the eight of us started to paddle across the endless grey water.

Everything started off smoothly. Sitting behind John, I could copy his pace and soon the four canoes were cutting smoothly across the waves, distracting my thoughts away from my fearful imagination. But then, suddenly. . .

Exercise 2

You find yourself washed ashore a deserted tropical island.

You have in your possession a sharp knife, a half-empty water bottle and a compass.

Make a list of things you could do during the next four hours before darkness falls.

Worksheet U
Sentence Construction

Teaching advice

In mainstream English lessons, sentence construction is covered in a variety of ways. This worksheet complements those lessons, providing additional focus on the subtle interaction of words, and the differing needs of written rather than spoken language. Dyslexic pupils commonly replace full stops with 'and then' (a tendency possibly reflected in their speech). Page 2 of the worksheet identifies these verbal full stops by leading the pupil(s) through sequential written instructions (providing reading experience).

In class

Read through the worksheet together ensuring that the pupil notes the different instructions on the first page. Read page 2 together, or let the pupil decode it alone, supporting the application of exercises that help identify the purpose and placement of full stops. The text illustrating the over-use of 'and then' is an example of scientific reporting. This provides the opportunity to discuss this form of writing, which dyslexic pupils commonly find very difficult to produce. The responses of the pupil both in class, and in their homework, identify the requirements of further inputs.

Worksheet U
Sentence Construction

Adaptive possibilities

- **Incorporate more punctuation**
  Commas, along with speech, exclamation and question marks, can be included in worksheets and discussed.

- **Utilise worksheets for reading practice**
  The shared introduction of worksheets extends the level of word decoding required, increasing the opportunity to include novel or unusual material.

- **Use the pupil's own work**
  Individual pupils may exhibit their own methods of creating passages that lack full stops. Reproduce a piece of the pupil's own writing for them to recognise either the over-use of 'and then', or their alternative.

- **Investigate the effect of sentences**
  Identical passages, varying only in the choice of short or united sentences, present different expressions of drama and emphasis. Short sentences develop suspense. Longer sentences slow down the pace of action.

Worksheet U1
Sentence Construction

Name:..

Date:................................... Form:............................

Draw lines to make meaningful sentences.

We left our	going to arrive?
The weather is	umbrellas at home.
When are we	behind.
She was left	wet and windy.

Choose one of the sentences you have made then write an additional sentence that *could* be found following it.

....

'Help !'	screamed John.
'I'm too old,'	asked the teacher.
'Good morning,'	purred the cat.
'Whose is this?'	groaned Grandpa.

Choose one of the sentences you have made then write an additional sentence that *could* be found before it.

....

When we speak, we tend not to leave spaces between our words. When we write, we always leave spaces between our words. Read the following words aloud:

'The boat hit a rock. It began to sink.'

Now repeat the words aloud, as if you were telling someone what happened, hearing the string of words, with a pause, which is where the full stop appears.
  Now read these words aloud:

'The boat hit a rock and then it began to sink.'

What replaces the full stop? ....

So, when you are writing, whenever you feel like writing 'and then', stop and consider if you want a full stop instead. Sometimes you will. Sometimes you won't.

Read through the following passage, crossing out 'and then' where you think a full stop would be better:

The apparatus was set up as shown in the diagram and then 5g of salt was added to the water and then the solution was stirred until it went clear and then another 5g of salt was added and then it was stirred again.

Worksheet V
Multiplication Tables

Teaching advice

Most dyslexic pupils find multiplication tables difficult to learn and retain over time. It is often better to provide a dyslexic pupil with a table square (and directions for use) to reduce the impact of rote-learning difficulties. Thus relieved, pupils will often begin to recognise and retain some of the multiplication patterns themselves, depending on usage, need and ability. Game-play develops familiarity of table factors and increases processing confidence, ability and speed.

In class

Complete page 1 of the worksheet to illustrate the usefulness of table knowledge. The drawing exercise brings $4 \times 4 = 16$ to life (memory enhancement). Utilise the sum to establish security. Over time, introduce and investigate different tables using colour, materials and art to boost inputs. Play the seven times table game. The game can be repeated as often as possible for homework.

Preparing for playing the game

Create two seven times table dice by labelling two dice with stickers or paint. The 12 faces depict values 7, 14, 21, 28, 35, 42, 49, 56, 63, 70, 3.5 and 700. Players throw one dice (either chosen by their opponent or from a bag), so distribute numbers randomly between dice. Photocopy the game board and provide counters for each player. Provide a table square if required.

Worksheet V
Multiplication Tables

Adaptive possibilities

• **Adapt for whole-class play or wet-weather play**

• **Use the four times table**
The dice are repainted to display numbers of feet and the game card includes lines such as:

| 6 elephants | 60 elephants | 9 elephants | half an elephant |

• **Use the eight times tables**
The dice are repainted to display numbers of tentacles and the game card includes lines such as:

| 12 octopuses | 3 octopuses | 7 octopuses | 5 octopuses |

• **Provide prizes for winning players**

Worksheet V1
Multiplication Tables

Name:..

Date:.. Form:..........................

1. How many days are there in three weeks?

   7 × 3 ....

2. To cook a chicken, place it in an oven preheated to 180°C/Gas Mark 4/350°F for 40 minutes per kg. If the chicken to be cooked weighs 4 kg, how long will it take to cook?

   4 × 40 = ... minutes

Knowing some sums by heart, e.g. 4 × 4 = 16 is very useful.

It is possible to find out 4 × 40 by working out

   4 × 40 = 40 + 40 + 40 + 40

but 4 × 40 = 4 × 4 × 10 is much quicker.

If Jim is given a car wheel on each birthday (!) by the time he is 16, he will have enough wheels for four cars. Draw Jim on his 16th birthday beside his four cars, each with four wheels and write the sum: 4 × 4 = 16.

There are a number of patterns within times tables. Look through the tables to see which ones conceal patterns.

The seven times table can be used to calculate days and weeks. Play this game to learn some multiplication.

START >>>>>	3 weeks	6 weeks	100 weeks	2 weeks
4 weeks	9 weeks	5 weeks	1 week	7 weeks
half a week	10 weeks	8 weeks	9 weeks	3 weeks
6 weeks	100 weeks	2 weeks	4 weeks	9 weeks
5 weeks	1 week	7 weeks	half a week	FINISH

Place your marker on START, then roll a seven times table dice. Then move your marker forwards one square.

Does the dice roll equal that square?

   NO: Move back one square.

   YES: Move forwards two squares.

Take it in turns to throw the dice and move a marker, or play the game on your own and time different games.

Worksheet W
Nonsense Words

Teaching advice

This worksheet presents invented words in order to develop and practise reading decoding skills. It enhances reading comprehension and word association skills, along with the presentation of genuine language for decoding experience and comprehension (e.g. 'cat's refuge').

Although the sheet may appear light-hearted, pupils with reading weaknesses will find some words more challenging than others, and, when further sheets are created, will need to continue to find some humour within the nonsense to maintain interest and success.

In class

Read through the worksheet together. Play with combinations of letters and the creation of new words: some short, some polysyllabic, some reflecting meaning. Identify whether pronunciation is good of sounds such as 'th', 'f' and 'v', and provide audio exercises such as:

> If 'dry' and 'smelly' = 'drelly', what do 'hot' and 'wet' equal?

The pupil should complete the worksheet for homework. Make extra sheets to practise further audio and visual decoding.

Worksheet W
Nonsense Words

Adaptive possibilities

- **Highlight visual patterns**
  Some words such as 'climb' and 'debt' require storage in the visual memory traces both for reading and spelling. A collection of 'odd bods' like these can be easily incorporated into sections of this worksheet.

- **Highlight meaning and implication**
  Many individual words (e.g. 'cow') do not possess an expressive meaning; you could never guess the meaning of the word 'cow' just from seeing or hearing it. But names reflecting character, and words from meaningful derivatives (e.g. 'displeasing') do display features within them that aid comprehension and expression. For pupils who have poor reading comprehension skills, focus on these aspects using both written and verbal delivery:

name of dragon	Inferno
infectious disease	spreadalitis

  Use the style of the worksheet to define terms such as

endangered species	(rareophyte)
dangerous specimen	(Predator Pete)

Worksheet W1
Nonsense Words

Name:...

Date:.. Form:............................

If you can read 'glad' and 'fight', you can read:

glight

To make it more interesting, choose a title from the right-hand list to match those on the left.

hairdresser	Ruff Justice
poodle parlour	Herr Kutz
grumpy lady	Smultch
guinea pig	Miss Frownly

dripping tap	plipperty plip
sticky stuff	'Meemeemee'
contented snail	gloopy
small child	slidling along

bird	Nibbly
lion	Flissing Fred
rabbit	Highroarer
snake	Cheeky Chirper

Here are some invented words. Draw a line to indicate the thing you think they are attached to:

cats' refuge

1.   Purrfect Hotel   cattery

vets' surgery

car repairs

2.   Kwik-Karpenters   carpet shop

woodworkers

name of ship

3.   Trixibella   name of pixie

name of tortoise

Invent some words to match the following:

1. A dinosaur ....

2. A delicious pudding ....

Worksheet X
Parts of Speech

Teaching advice

Playing a game is one of the best ways to get information into long-term memory. The element of competition encourages application and allows for repetitive inputs without boring the pupil. Providing meaningful prompts to terms such as 'pronoun' develops reliable memory traces that are sustainable over time.

Prompts add depth to a memory trace. Dyslexics often find they can remember things for only a short period of time; you can establish the meaning of 'common noun' in Tuesday's lesson, but by Friday the pupils are confusing it with 'pronoun'. Prompts are therefore necessary inclusions for secure long-term memory traces to be established.

In class

Begin with page 2 of the worksheet, introducing and explaining the meaning of the (confusing) term 'parts of speech'. Go through the terms 'noun', 'proper noun', etc., but not their definitions. This begins to familiarise the pupil with the key words. Then play the Parts of Speech game with the pupil. Play the game repeatedly over a week, and test definitions and prompts (which may have been adapted to suit individual pupils). Success helps pupils to recognise the value of meaningful prompts. Use the terms 'verb', etc. in other work to establish familiarity.

Playing the Parts of Speech game

The first time a definition is required (e.g. adverb), turn over the sheet and examine the explanation and prompts. In the case of 'adverb', the definition of 'verb' will also need attending to.

The second and subsequent times a definition is required, see if the pupil can recall the prompt that helps to identify a definition (e.g. pronoun – professional footballer, substitute), and use the table of definitions to confirm/reinforce the prompt.

Worksheet X
Parts of Speech

Adaptive possibilities

- **Adapt prompts to suit individuals**
  If 'verb' is causing difficulty, add depth by searching for verbs that begin with a 'v': to visit, to view, to vaccinate, to voice, to vibrate. Then let the pupil create their own prompt using one of these verbs.

- **Vary the arrangement of key words**
  In another game reorganise the layout so that an adverb is required when a 2 is thrown on the dice. This variation ensures that memory traces are not attached to numbers or placement in table.

- **Add additional parts of speech**
  In another game introduce 'collective noun', 'conjunction', etc. Encourage the pupil to devise their own meaningful prompts, ensuring that they connect the key word to a definition in an appropriate way.

- **Use other key words**
  Collect the key words required to label a flower/volcano/boat. Discuss each term and devise a prompt for terms whose meaning are difficult to remember (e.g. 'port' means 'left', and both have four letters). Players are then presented with a picture and must label it according to the throws on the dice. The first one to complete the labelling wins.

- **Use pictorial prompts**
  Pictorial displays are often more easily recalled than words and can convey meaning that would otherwise be confusing to explain. The meaning of the term 'conjunction' can be highlighted by the pupil turning some of the letters into large roads. Write a short sentence in each road. Surround the picture with words such as 'and', 'so', 'because' which could be used to connect the individual sentences.

Worksheet X1
Parts of Speech

Name:..

Date:.. Form:..........................

A game for two players

1	Proper noun		
2	Common noun		
3	Pronoun		
4	Adjective		
5	Adverb		
6	Throw again		

Take it in turns to throw a dice. Write down an appropriate word. The first player to fill in three words in one box is the winner.

Play this game a number of times over one week.

Play the game three weeks later to test your memory.

Adapt the game to learn other key words.

Worksheet X1
Page 2

Attaching prompts to the meaning of key words

It is important to know the meaning of the term 'parts of speech'. This term means the part played by a word in a particular sentence.

Example

A <u>frown</u> uses more muscles than a smile. (common noun)
She <u>frowned</u> at the cat, but it took no notice. (verb)

Noun	A noun is a thing. A noun is an object. A 'town' is a noun.	e.g. The <u>town</u> is big.
Proper noun	There are different types of noun. A 'proper noun' is the **name** of something. It **always** begins with a **capital** letter.	e.g. <u>London</u> is big.
Common noun	Another type of noun is a 'common noun'. This is a noun that does not start with a capital letter, but it does not have to be a common word (the term 'common' is confusing).	e.g. He had never seen a <u>computer</u> before.
Pronoun	A pronoun is in place of a noun. (When a professional footballer is injured, a **substitute** is put in his/her place.)	e.g. He scored a goal. <u>They</u> cheered and <u>we</u> groaned.
Verb	A verb is a doing word.	e.g. We <u>viewed</u> the sky through a telescope.
Adjective	An adjective **adds** to the meaning of a noun. (A noun is an object; an adjective tells you more about it.)	e.g. He bought his dad an <u>adjustable</u> spanner.
Adverb	An adverb **adds** to the meaning of a verb. (Add-to-verb = adverb.)	e.g. He closed the door <u>quietly</u>.

Worksheet Y
Choosing the Odd One Out

Teaching advice

This worksheet tackles a familiar exercise but highlights the common difficulty that dyslexic pupils often encounter when merely asked to identify 'the odd one out'. Through the application of lateral thinking skills, dyslexic pupils can often make unpredicted (but valid) associations between words. For example, asked to choose the odd one out of 'oak', 'fir', 'sycamore' and 'daffodil', a dyslexic pupil might say 'fir, because it has leaves all the year round'.

Through practice and discussion, pupils can be encouraged to consider a variety of different answers before choosing 'the most likely' one with respect to the strength of association between linked words. Mistakes can be made through an erroneous belief that overly 'clever' answers are required, through the misreading/comprehending of words, and through rapid decisions made without due consideration of alternative possibilities.

In class

Use this sheet as a reading and word comprehension exercise. Assess approach, application and nature of lateral thinking skills. Answers are only wrong if the pupil is unable to justify their selection.

Worksheet Y
Choosing the Odd One Out

Adaptive possibilities

- **Exercise different senses**
  Challenging the memories of taste, smell and touch along with visual, audio and semantic associations, highlights and strengthens memory processing skills.

- **Use the worksheet to develop word comprehension**

recess	minute	vert	kilogram
concave	microscopic	blanc	litre
cupped	massive	chien	inch
convex	minuscule	noir	fossil fuel

- **Use the worksheet to develop reading skills**

exceptional	lightening	road	metre
unimportant	lightning	rowed	litre
insignificant	bleaching	rode	centre
irrelevant	blanching	travelled	acre

- **Encourage pupils to explore word associations**

associate with colour: SNOW similarities: .... differences:	associate with heat: SNOW similarities: .... differences: ....

Worksheet Y1
Choosing the Odd One Out

Name:..

Date:.................................... Form:........................

Circle the odd one out (according to meaning):

rubbish	pizza	happiness
treasure	mushroom	jewellery
scrap	carrot	jealousy
worthless	tomato	despair

Circle the odd one out (according to taste):

lemon	chocolate mousse and cream
sugar	vanilla ice-cream and banana
chocolate	apples in cinnamon and ginger sauce
honey	lemon bombe and raspberry sauce

Circle the odd one out (according to sound):

car	mosquito	violin concerto
aeroplane	dripping tap	singing canary
bee	clock	smoke alarm
snail	hand clapping	carol singing

growl	thud	meow	hee-haw

Circle the odd one out (according to touch):

silver spoon	mud	volcanic lava
cat's fur	milk	boiling water
cotton wool	yoghurt	lemon bombe
velvet	biscuits	hot chocolate drink

Circle the odd one out (according to appearance):

lemon bombe and raspberry sauce	a snail's egg
buttercups and poppies	the world
blackberries and snowdrops	yoghurt
red cherries and custard	a tennis ball

Fill in similarities and differences:

by meaning: LION
similar: …………… ……………
different: …………… ……………

by touch: POPCORN
similar: …………… ……………
different: …………… ……………

by smell: SCENTED ROSE
similar: …………… ……………
different: …………… ……………

by meaning: UNICORN
similar: …………… ……………
different: …………… ……………

Worksheet Z
Spelling by Number

Teaching advice

Games are an excellent way of achieving learning. Their novelty allows varied application and repetition.

This 'simple' game contains elements specifically designed to support the dyslexic learning style with the use of colour, backward word-spelling (uses visual memory), focus on vowels, and a graphic-spatial task being just some ways of developing memory traces.

Games can also include aspects of scoring (calculating and recording numbers) and instructions that need to be read, followed and understood.

In class

Gather the equipment needed. Provide each pupil with two copies of the worksheet to make the instructions easier to follow. Introduce the game, helping pupils to read and understand the guidelines (use it as a reading decoding and comprehension exercise). Start the game and then calculate their 'base score' accordingly.

Use a variety of words. Long ones will need to be chunked into smaller parts when spelled backwards. Note areas of difficulty. Play the game for homework.

Worksheet Z
Spelling by Number

Adaptive possibilities

- **Subject-based vocabulary**
  - Geographical terminology (e.g. continental drift) can be learnt through presenting piles of 12 varied words. When pupils read a word, they must explain it too.
  - Historical dates, numbers in a multiplication table, telephone numbers and birthdays can be similarly memorised. Add pictures or phrases to prompt association.
  - Second languages, spelling patterns and revision word-lists also share a need for multisensory, repetitive inputs.

- **Variations of the task**
  Depending on their individual learning style, pupils will find some tasks difficult and others easy. Apportioning different tasks to the dice throws provides varied exercises for the visual, audio, semantic (word meaning and association) and kinesthetic channels. Others could include:

  Write with 'opposite' hand.

  Sing letters.

  Use bubble-writing.

  Spell word while hopping.

- **Pupil extension**
  Pupils are encouraged to adapt this game themselves.

Worksheet Z1
Spelling by Number

Name:..

Date:.................................... Form:...........................

This is a spelling game. It uses a dice, a pile of 12 words written out on separate cards, some plain paper for writing on, coloured pens and a timer.

- Look at a word.

- Move the word out of sight.

- Throw the dice.

- Then follow the instructions below.

1	Write the word in capitals.
2	Spell the word, aloud, backwards.
3	Write the word making every letter a different colour.
4	Draw a box, and write the word to fill the box perfectly.
5	Use a red pen for every vowel.
6	Write the word with your eyes closed.

Worksheet Z1
Page 2

Work through your pile of words, noting the time whenever six words are spelled correctly.

If a word is spelled incorrectly, it is shuffled into the master pile for re-use. If a word is spelled correctly, it goes to the bottom of a second pile.

Select the next word from the top of alternate piles.

Continue until six words have been spelled correctly.

Note the time. Calculate your score (see below).

This game will help you to learn French vocabulary, scientific terms, key words in history, etc. as well as words for an English spelling test.

When you first play this game, find out how long it takes you to accurately spell four words: ………. minutes

This time is your 'base time'.

When you play the game for the second time (when six words need to be spelled correctly), you can deduct your base time from the time it takes you to complete the task.

When you beat your base time, move on to new words.

| base time: | | 2nd game: | | 4th game: | |
| 1st game: | | 3rd game: | | 5th game: | |

Index
Which Dragonfly Worksheet?

Dragonfly Worksheets can be used to develop the following skills:

Skill	A	B	C	D	E	F	G	H	I	J	K	L	M	N	O	P	Q	R	S	T	U	V	W	X	Y	Z
Short-term visual memory	A	B	C		E			H		J	K		M	N		P	Q	R	S		U	V	W	X		Z
Short-term audio memory	A	B	C	D	E		G	H	I	J	K		M			P	Q	R	S			V	W	X		Z
word association		B			E	F	G	H		J	K	L		N			Q	R	S		U		W	X	Y	
Penmanship						F	G			J		L	M		O		Q	R	S		U					Z
Copying		B			E		G	H		J									S							
Single-word reading	A		C		E			H		J	K			N				R	S				W	X	Y	Z
Reading comprehension	A	B		D	E	F	G	H	I		K	L		N		P	Q	R		T	U		W		Y	
Spelling	A	B	C		E	F	G	H	I	J		L	M	N	O			R	S				W			Z
Sequencing									I	J					O	P	Q			T		V				
Processing speed				D		F										P		R				V				Z
Numeracy														N		P	Q	R				V				
Sentence construction							G		I			L	M		O					T	U			X		
Written composition									I			L			O				S	T						
Second languages	A	B				F				J	K		M					R	S		U				Y	Z